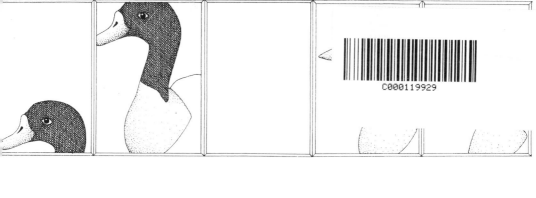

I never travel without my diary. One should always have something sensational to read in the train.

oscar wilde

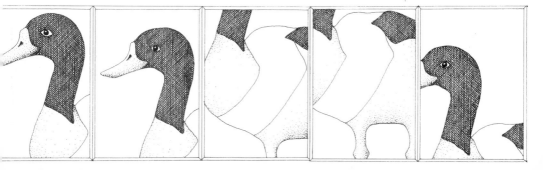

THE DUCK
STOPS HERE

trust me
I'm a ducktor

ANTIQUE COLLECTORS' CLUB

to Caroline
and
everyone in the book-in-hand club

...so you must be Drake

drew

©1998 Simon Drew
World copyright reserved

ISBN 1 85149 290 9

British Library Cataloguing-in-Publication Data
A catalogue record for this book is available from the British Library

Published and printed in England by the Antique Collectors' Club Ltd., Woodbridge, Suffolk
on Consort Royal Era Satin from Donside Mill, Aberdeen, Scotland

Cedric
was always
on his mobile fawn

3

A Letter from a Stilted Duck called Elvis

I don't have a wooden heart
so love me tender,
and if this letter's not so smart
return to sender:
said the stilted duck called Elvis.

You'll never walk alone, not quite:
just find my doorway.
And if you're lonesome, dear, tonight
just do it your way,
said the stilted duck called Elvis.

This thread of life is taut and fine
and easy to sever
and I don't care if the sun don't shine
it's now or never
said the stilted duck called Elvis.

large duck with rook sack

Not everything is what it seems
Here's the biscuit queen
Biscuit dreams

Custard creams
Nothing can dislodge her
(Jammy dodger)

ORGANISM ROAMINGS
(or TOEDANCE ANECDOTE)

In search of the anagrammatic trophy

which is revealed at the end, for the reader to discover.

bradfield

horris

① One young hero's name was Horris,
Bradfield was his friend:
they aimed to trace a secret password
to the bitter end.

② With this password safely gathered
they might rule the earth
taking fees from those with wealth
to those of humble birth.

③First they travelled in their costume
  (each end of a horse)
  finding strange contorted creatures
  as they neared the source.

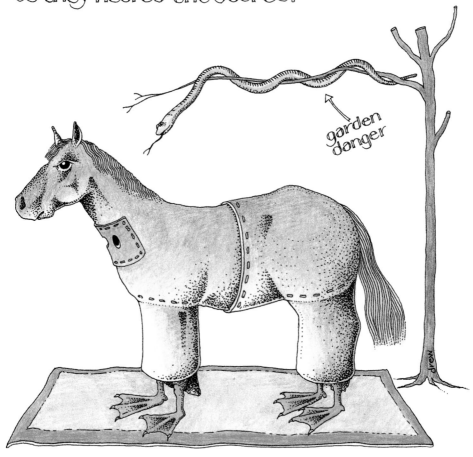

garden
danger

④Bradfield lead the first adventure
  Horris took the rear:
  both would shout for port and starboard,
  both would try to steer.

11

⑤ Soon they found a fount of felines
 coolest ocelots:
 these were cats with furry coats on
 buttons, zips and spots.

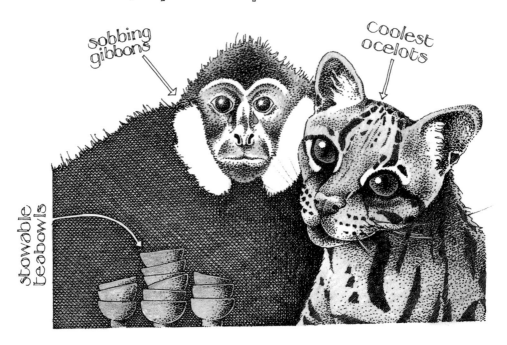

sobbing
gibbons

coolest
ocelots

stowable
teabowls

⑥ Sobbing gibbons gave them signals:
 a desert would be crossed.
 Here they found the chained echidna
 (we thought they'd all been lost).

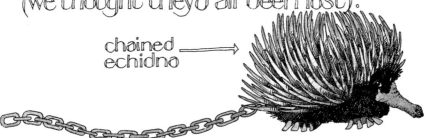

chained
echidna

straying
stingray

⑦ Underwater straying stingrays:
   they looked for every one.
   Our seastorm maestros fished the oceans,
   their bait - a current bun.

mid-ocean
comedian

seastorm
maestros

13

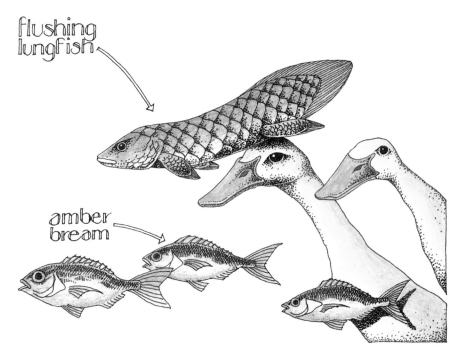

flushing
lungfish

amber
bream

⑧ The flushing lungfish lives in Egypt,
the home of amber bream.
(The bargepole porbeagle lives there too,
though up a different stream).

bargepole
porbeagle

14

seawater
teawares

seabird
airbeds

barnacle
balancer

rectal
claret

⑨ Seabird airbeds bobbed like ice floes
   on rectal claret seas:
   this is where the chinese rice grows
   and hornets' thrones have knees.

hornets'
thrones

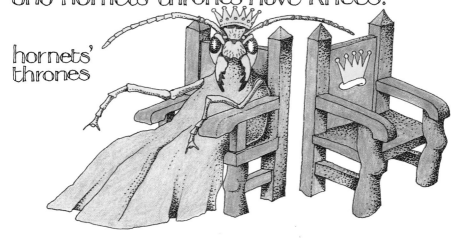

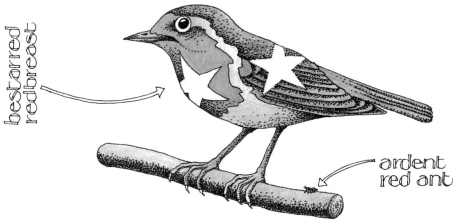

bestarred
redbreast

ardent
red ant

⑩ Once they found a bestarred redbreast
hiding in a log :
painless spaniels stole its bird nest
(the grounded underdog).

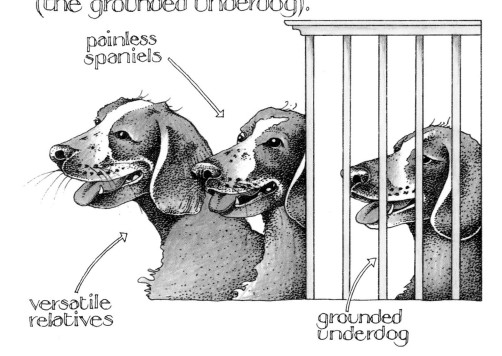

painless
spaniels

versatile
relatives

grounded
underdog

⑪ A carthorse orchestra played sweet music
   (although it's just pretend).
   Still no passwords: still no secrets:
   still no journey's end.

carthorse
orchestra →

⑫ But as they felt depressed, defeated
   and turned back home for sleep,
   there the passwords grinned like kittens
   rising from the deep.

drew

17

duck with my newt (detail)

Fraternally Entwined

1
I once knew a pair of ducklings,
their mother's pride and joy.
Both of them were little girls
except for the little boy.

2
I once knew a pair of ducklings,
their mother's joy and pride.
Clichés shouldn't be reversed;
(it's like a groom and bride).

3
I once knew a pair of ducklings,
the joy and pride of mother:
they made such charming sisters
(except that one's a brother).

4
(I once knew a pair of ducklings
a mother's pride was theirs;
she'd other ducklings in her nest
but thought of them as spares).

21

pigeon-towed duck

For whom the leather worker
makes boots with leather soles?
For whom he makes the handbag?
For whom the belt holes?

ONE PRISONER TO ANOTHER

① How will we escape this board?
Fight up every rung?
To find an anaconda's scored:
we're wrenched from where we clung.

24

And every time we think we're floored
we feel like we've been stung,
but climb back up for our reward:
a python's flicking tongue.

25

② And here's another game we play
   with pawns and knights and kings
   always getting in our way
   when we want better things.

So will this chess game ever end?
The board's become a wreck.
Is your plumage tweed, my friend?
Or would you call it check, (mate)?

A Woolley Ode

Carefree and aimless
a runner duck appeared,
righteous pure and blameless
others thought it weird.
Leaving in a puff of smoke
it never said a word,
never did explain the joke -
elusive irksome bird.

MATER AND PATER

Childhood days: the best you've had.
And even when you're slightly bad
they make you cheerful when you're sad.
They tuck you up, your mum and dad.

29

THE DELIVERY

These ducks are from Calcutta
        and they're trying to escape:
their beaks cut wood like butter
        though they're hopeless with red tape.
They've often seen rough oceans
        but they'll soon be on a calmer sea.

The brushes come with lotions
        and they're destined for a pharmacy,

with soaps and hair restorers.

(The box is just Pandora's).

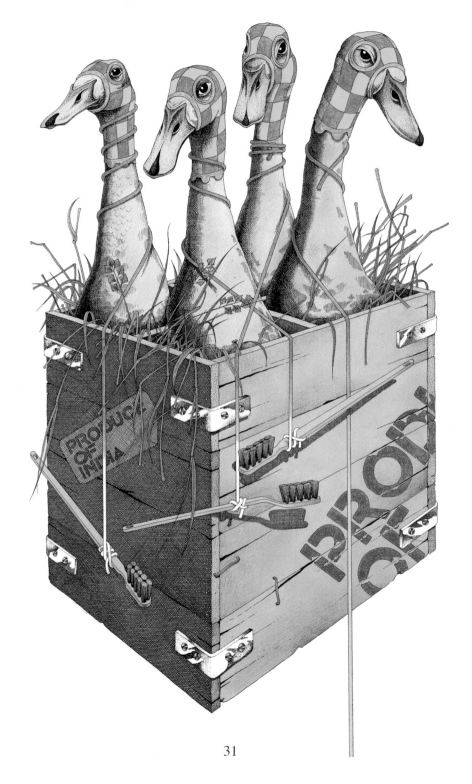

THE END OF ROGER

It's called Start Point: it's jagged rock,
and on it sits a lighthouse
warning sailors round the clock –
this pointed, flashing whitehouse.

All night long its ceaseless flame
advertises danger,
blinking like a childish game
to startle friend or stranger.

Upon that crag a call-duck perched,
an ancient cliff-ledge lodger,
and though he'd never really searched
he'd found his name was Roger.

His sweet short life was suffered here
beneath that glowing beacon
and, reader, you may shed a tear:
his heart began to weaken.

He knew that as he neared his death
the lighthousemen adored him
and just before his final breath
his whole life flashed before him.

'If I cannot smoke in heaven
then I shall not go.'
mark twain

THE IMMACULATE CONFECTION

They chop up apples every day
They peel and pip and core them
There's Jill and Joy from Maidenhead,
This work will never bore them.

They chop up apples every day:
there's Norah, Sue and Brenda
and as they toil they chant and pray
for Christ's on their agenda.

They chop up apples every day
the pastry factory beavers
and while they cook their pies and cakes
they're God's dessert believers.

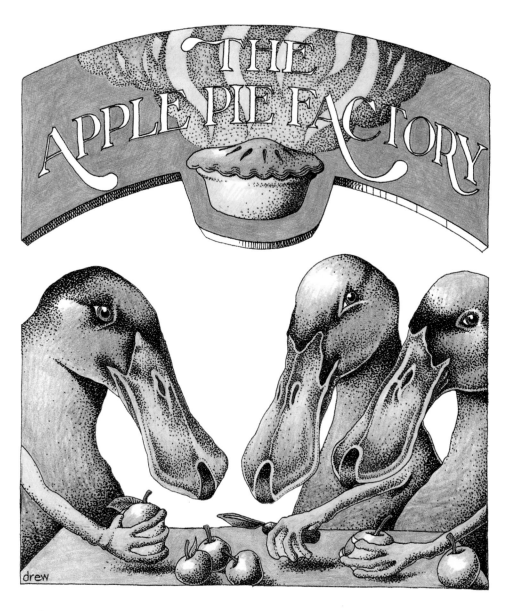

They chop up apples every day;
these Jills and Joys and Norahs.
And all the time they're singing hymns:
the Hallelujah corers.

THE QUEEN OF FISH

Which came first:
   the chicken or the fish?
Which came first:
   the dinner or the dish?
      To make you thinner,
       it's the fish and dinner.
Which came first:
   the duck or its egg?
Which came first:
   the trouser or the leg?
      To make you beg,
       it would be a (bent) leg.
Which came first:
   the queen or the card?
Which came first:
   the sonnet or the bard?
      If you want a crown on it
       it's the queen and sonnet.
Which came first:
   the enemy or friend?
Which came first:
   the middle or

THE END

and there he stood. . . .

tall duck and handsome

'golf is a good walk ruined'
mark twain

examples of duck humour:

'I always keep a supply of stimulant handy
in case I see a snake,
which I also keep handy.' w.c.fields.

45

duck be my lady tonight

Famous Indian Composers

HAYDN SIKH

bring on the clones

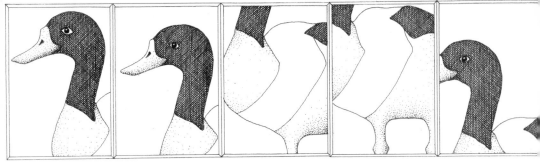

Nothing that is worth knowing
can be taught.

oscar wilde

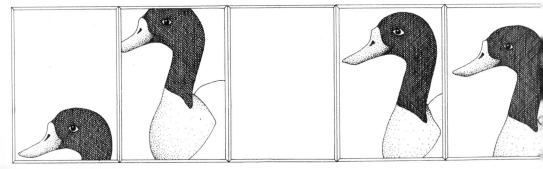